LOCAL TRAVEL GUIDE TO BELARUS

ANNA MARTSYNKEVICH

OPPIAN

Published by Oppian Press
Helsinki, Finland

ISBN 978-951-877-183-1

CONTENTS

Welcome to Belarus   1

Belarusian cuisine   12

Transport in Belarus   18

Castles of Belarus   24

Nature of Belarus   32

Orthodox churches   38

Catholic churches   42

War history tourism   46

Ethno-tourism   51

Sports in Belarus   53

Art museums   56

Museums and places dedicated to famous people   59

Romantic places to visit as a couple   66

Other famous sights that you'll love   70

Miscellaneous tips and facts   76

WELCOME TO BELARUS

BELARUS IS A COUNTRY LOCATED IN EASTERN EUROPE THAT NOT TOO many people have heard much about, especially those who are not from Europe. Nevertheless, this doesn't make Belarus a less fascinating place. In fact, people who haven't heard of it are missing out on a lot of good stuff!

Belarus is famous for its beautiful nature and wildlife, specifically forests, wide picturesque plains, and numerous lakes. It's often poetically called "the blue-eyed land" among the locals, referring to a large number of lakes and other water bodies spread around the country's landscape. The beauty of local nature has always been valued, and it was sang with love by Belarusian poets, writers, musicians, and painters for many years. There are five national parks across the country, and one of them, Belavezhskaya Pushcha, is listed by UNESCO as World Heritage Site and Biosphere Reserve.

Another poetic name for Belarus is "the land under the white wings", which refers to the large population of storks, one of the national symbols. Storks are believed to bring good luck and they can be often seen in the countryside during any road trip, even on major highways.

Traveling to Belarus would also be a treat for those who look for ethno-tourism, rural tourism, historical landmarks, World War II memorial places, Soviet architecture, sports activities and events, or just an entirely different culture to dive into and explore. The architecture of Belarus is mostly made in Soviet style and there are very few spots of classic old European locations due to the fact that Belarus really suffered during World War II and most of it was completely destroyed. But this kind of "look" is what makes this country unique in its own way, giving you the vibe that you may not be typically used to.

Citizens of Belarus are believed to be very friendly, peaceful, and hospitable. Doing their best to make a good impression on their guests and make the guests feel at home is a huge part of Belarusian mentality. The patience and peacefulness of the locals stem from the nation's history, and that's what made Belarusians value their peace. Belarus is friendly towards all of its visitors and is always interested in sharing its culture and traditions while making everyone feel welcome.

Why not Belorussia?

In many countries and languages, the name of Belarus is literally translated as "White Russia". Local citizens can find it quite offensive, since this country has changed its name from Belorussia, "white Russia", to the Republic of Belarus in 1991, after the collapse of the USSR and after Belarus has established its independence. So it would be best to call it Belarus no matter where you're from because Belorussia stopped existing many years ago.

Local climate

The climate of Belarus is temperate-continental with moderate features, having warm (sometimes hot) summers and cold humid winters with abundant snowfalls. It's influenced by airwaves from the

Atlantic, and the weather can be a little unstable. This kind of climate is typical for Central Europe.

What time of year is best for visiting Belarus? There are two times of the year when Belarus looks the best: in summer, with all of its greenness and spectacular nature, and around Christmas and New Year's celebrations when everything in big cities is decorated with holiday lights. There is a high chance of getting a nice snowfall during the winter celebrations, which adds a lot of points to the magical holiday atmosphere. Lots of festivals, open-air gigs and parties are held during summertime and very early autumn, and wintertime around Christmas is full of parties and celebrations, including open-air skating rinks, if the weather allows that.

Even if you check the weather forecast before your trip, consider taking an extra hoodie with you, especially in the wintertime. The humid climate makes everything feel colder (and in summer – warmer) than it really is. During winter, warm and waterproof footwear is an absolute must.

Do you need a visa?

In fact, if you are a mere traveler, you might not need a visa at all. There is a big list of countries whose citizens don't need a visa to travel to Belarus at all, and for others, there still are some restrictions. According to the law that was adopted in July of 2018, there are visa-free travel programs that you can choose from.

Foreign citizens can stay in Belarus up to 30 days if they arrive there by air into Minsk National Airport. These rules will not work if you're arriving by air from Russia (and for those who are flying to Russia as well) since this is considered an internal flight with no border control. Visa-free entry doesn't apply to those who arrive for working, business, or studying purposes if their periods of activity are over 30 days.

There are also two special visa-free zones that you can stay in up to 10 days without a visa. They are located in Brest region and Grodno region, including the cities of Brest and Grodno themselves. To be able to stay in Grodno region you will need to visit the Augustow Canal Park, and if your purpose is the Belavezhskaya Pushcha national park, you'll be able to stay in Brest region. This will give you more than enough time to see the sights in the said zones and enjoy the local hospitality.

Emergency numbers in Belarus

The emergency number for the Belarusian rescue and fire department is 101;

Police number is 102;

Ambulance number is 103;

Emergency gas service number (in case of the gas smell or any suspicions) is 104;

The Ministry of Emergency Situations hotline number is 112.

All of the listed numbers are free of charge and can be dialed from both cell and landline phones.

Languages of Belarus

Belarus has two official languages – Russian and Belarusian, which seemingly should sound similar, yet they don't. The fun fact is that lots of Russian-speaking people can't understand Belarusian at all if they haven't studied it specifically. But even if you don't know any of these two languages, it's more than possible to navigate in the famous touristic places of Belarus if you have basic knowledge of English. It may get a little harder to communicate with the locals if you go somewhere off the beaten path, but that's usually not an issue, but instead an extra adventure for those travelers who prefer exploring the places on their own. In the touristic places, the necessary information and all of the signs are written in English, and you can book guided tours in English as well.

In Minsk, the capital city, all of the signs that are meant for the foreigners are written in Belarusian and duplicated in English for easy understanding, and the stations in the subway are announced in these two languages as well. In the touristic center of the city, most of the service personnel are capable of communicating in English pretty decently, and younger generations of Belarusians also speak it well enough to answer your possible questions. So you don't have to worry about it at all.

Local money and tax-free system

You can pay for the purchases and services by credit and debit cards of international payment systems. There shouldn't be any problems with it in big cities. Here's an advice, though: it would be best if you carry some cash - Belarusian rubles - with you, especially if you plan to go exploring the country somewhere away from the most popular sights. In the shopping centers, there always are currency exchange booths and a cash machine or two (or more, belonging to several different banks). Exchange booths accept USD, Euro, and Russian rubles everywhere, and some banks can accept less widespread currencies as well.

The Belarusian ruble, BYN for short, isn't fully convertible currency, therefore you won't be able to get any of it before you get into the country itself. You can probably find Belarusian rubles in some banks in Russia (in Moscow, Saint Petersburg, or Smolensk), and in other neighboring countries of Belarus, especially in those which are popular shopping destinations for the Belarusians, but it would be much easier to get local currency right there. BYN is a rather new abbreviation that replaced BYR after the redenomination in the summer of 2016. Before the redenomination, there were no coins in circulation in the history of independent Belarus. There were commemorative coins released specifically for tourists and coin collectors, but they, of course, were never used as a currency. However, now the official currency of Belarus is available in both banknotes (5, 10, 20, 50, 100, 200, and 500 rubles) and coins (1, 2, 5, 10, 20, 50 kopecks, 1 and 2 rubles). 1 and 2 ruble coins' designs look very similar to euros, so don't mix them up!

It would be fair to say that the prices in Belarus are lower than in many other European countries due to the local economy. You might be surprised by how cheap public transport is, or how easy it is to visit touristic attractions without spending a fortune. Moreover, the tax-free system will help you get back the VAT on the purchases that you made in Belarus unless you are a member of the Eurasian Economic Union, so spend away! You can get the Tax Free cash refund at certain Belarusbank offices before departing from Belarus. To be able to do it, however, you should do the following things:

- Purchase at least BYN 80 worth of goods in one store within a single day using the tax-free system, keep your goods unused and in undamaged packaging;

- Get three copies of your tax-free receipt from the store, using a passport or any other equivalent document;

- Take the original tax-free receipt and one copy of it to the customs service in a special prepaid envelope;

- Prepare your receipts and show them at the border checking point as you leave Belarus to get a special seal at the customs;

- Use the receipt to fill in the documents, put it into your prepaid envelope, and after that, you'll have to either put it into a mailbox at the border checkpoint or mail it later from your (or other) country within six months after you have exported your purchased goods from Belarus.

That's actually easier than it sounds, so just remember to get three copies of your tax-free receipts, keep your purchases untouched, and visit the Tax-Free office at Belarusbank before leaving. You can always find more information here or on the internet, so don't worry, just think about all the goods that you'll bring home!

What to bring home

You can buy and enjoy a huge variety of goods made in Belarus, from traditional local souvenirs with unique Belarusian character and a long history behind them to regular everyday goods of high quality.

Souvenirs

Flax has been grown and cultivated in Belarus since ancient times. The fibers and seeds of flax were used in almost everything, and it's no wonder that the blue flowers of flax are a part of the national emblem of Belarus. Flax is an environmentally-friendly, trendy and very versatile material – it can be turned into either coarse or soft fabric, depending on what purpose it's going to serve. Flax seeds were used to make kisel (see Belarusian drinks) and uniquely tasting the bread. What kind of flax-related souvenirs can you find? Clothes, bedclothes, tablecloths and table napkins, decorated with all kinds of embroidery, bath and sauna towels – any textile product you can imagine. Look for the brands named Blakit and Belarusian Linen. There also are lovely decorative dolls made of flax, that are believed to be amulets for good luck and money.

Another ancient craft of the local people is making goods out of sheep wool. Felt hats and special felt boots called valenki (they are a famous Russian souvenir as well) were irreplaceable for the villagers during harsh winter times. And even though modern technologies allow to create clothes that have warmer material and are easier to make (at least, not with bare hands), handcrafted felt accessories and boots are still highly valued, especially as unique and memorable souvenirs. The old town named Dribin still preserves the felting traditions from the 18th century, so if you want to get yourself a unique and authentic pair of valenki, you know where to look.

Straw was widely used as a building material, as well as a very beautiful material for making art. Wreaths, dolls, and simple bundles of straw were used in Belarusian folk rituals and the making of famous iconostases. It symbolizes the energy of the sun and has an incredible shiny golden color. You can find such souvenirs as straw figurines of all sorts, shoes, and hats made of straw (straw hats are a very typical part of Belarusian national costumes), pretty boxes, accessories, and amulets, that are believed to protect your home and ensure the well-being of your family. Wooden souvenirs are often decorated with straw as well.

Osier or willow branches were used on Belarusian territory in ancient times for making fences and even house walls, cribs for the babies, and durable baskets (babies were sometimes put into the baskets too). Modern craftsmen still make many of these things with their hands, and osier fences are still a popular thing in the villages. You can purchase osier furniture, baskets, some types of kitchen utensils, or traditional bast sandals of the ancient villagers – lapty. They surely aren't too practical nowadays but will make a great souvenir and important addition to a national Belarusian costume, if you're interested in owning one.

Slutsk belts are one of the most remarkable and well-known Belarusian symbols, a true national treasure. Slutsk is the name of the town they were produced in. They were worn exclusively by noblemen, symbolizing their wealth and status, since they were very expensive. The technology was originally brought from Oriental countries in the 18th century and the manufactory continued until the middle of the 19th century. They were made of silk threads and could be one- two- three- or four-facial for them to be worn on different occasions, depending on the color. The color was visible after folding the belt. Modern belts have this feature as well and can actually be a part of an outfit in boho style or something similar to it. The original Slutsk belts are now a rarity stored in museums and private collections, but several years ago the unique tradition was revived, and modern craftsmen produce the exact copies of the old belts. Don't you think it would make an amazing exclusive souvenir?

Wooden souvenirs are eco-friendly and widely used in modern interior design. Wooden utensils, chests, boxes, figurines, and carved furniture are widely available in Belarus.

Glass and crystalware have been made in Belarus for over a hundred years. Neman Glass Works and Borisov Crystal Factory are the most famous factories that provide the finest high-quality items. You can purchase all sorts of tableware, candle holders, various figurines, and even stained glass. Even if it's hard to export and transport, it would be worth it if you appreciate that kind of art.

Ceramics have a much longer history and are an ancient craft. Each craftsman used to have their own secrets and artistic approach. Ceramicware was (and can be) used for storing milk and other foods, and some traditional music instruments of Belarus were made out of clay. The most famous are small flutes, bells, and whistles that are shaped like different animals. If you're not interested in music, there's a

9

large variety of decorative figurines, candleholders, fridge magnets, and crockery. Another true Belarusian gifts are ceramic products from the town of Radoshkovichi. They produce tableware and various interior decorations. By the way, traditional dishes of Belarusian cuisine are much better when cooked in clay pots.

The souvenirs can also be edible. For example, Belarusian candies made by Krasny Pischevik, Spartak, and Kommunarka confectioneries, are healthy and delicious, and they would make a perfect gift from Belarus. Unfortunately, it wouldn't work for vegans. Among zephyr, marmalade and regular chocolate candies you can also find liquor candies with fillings that taste like Belarusian berries.

Alcohol from Belarus in special gift packaging would also be a great gift. High-quality balsams, liquors, and vodka in souvenir bottles and bags not only taste good but also look fantastic.

Other goods

Linen clothes aren't the only strong side of Belarus. Local knitwear, lingerie, and cotton clothes are also highly popular among visitors from different countries. Even though some people find the clothing design of some Belarusian brands boring, several brands produce high-quality goods of the European level. Mark Formelle, Serge, and Milavitsa make outstanding lingerie and underwear, Conte is a famous hosiery brand, Marusya create beautifully designed clothes for kids and young teenagers, Svitanok and Kupalinka are well-known for their knitwear.

Footwear and accessory manufacturers from Belarus are trusted by the customers due to the quality of their materials. Marko and Luch produce regular footwear for men and women, ShagoVita is known for the kids' shoes, Belkelme – for the sports' shoes, Galanteya and Mattiolli are local brands that make good bags and leather accessories.

Belarusian cosmetic brands are very well-known in the neighboring countries due to the quality and affordability of their goods that are made with the use of organic components. Belita and Vitex are the leading brands in this industry, creating endless new formulas and recipes of different cosmetics for various purposes, including professional ones. If you're looking for make-up, try BelorDesign and Relouis.

BELARUSIAN CUISINE

Food

Of course, you can eat in a pizzeria, in a restaurant that serves Asian food or in any other regular café, if you want. But let's face the truth: did you really come all the way to Belarus to eat the same dishes you can have in any other country? Who needs pizza or Caesar salad when you can have machanka and draniki with sour cream the way it won't be served anywhere else?

Local cuisine was influenced mostly by the following two factors: active farming and extensive usage of local produce, and a huge influence from neighboring countries and migrant settlers. Belarus has always had good relationships with the neighboring countries, and people of many nations have chosen it as a place to live. Since the times of the Grand Duchy of Lithuania, the national culinary traditions have united Baltic, German, Jewish, and Slavic cuisine and created an exciting mix. Old Belarusian recipes have survived to the present day, lots of local citizens use them in their daily diet, and the visitors of Belarus always show a huge interest in these dishes. The restaurants that serve traditional Belarusian food can offer you not only the simple recipes that were used by commoners in the countryside but also sophisticated dishes of the nobility – using modern ways of cooking, of course. These restaurants also have an authentic good-looking interior design full of local color and curious details. If you're interested in ethno-tourism, the touristic farmsteads are serving traditional dishes that are common for their particular areas, made with fresh farm produce.

The local produce used in Belarusian cuisine can be divided into the following categories (so that you'd know what to expect):

- Various vegetables and greens that are typical for the local climate, either homegrown or purchased – turnips, beets, carrots, cabbages, potatoes, cucumbers, pumpkins, and others;

- Fruits and berries, also typical for the climate and the landscape, including wild berries. Some of the examples are apples, cherries, currants, blackberries, blueberries, and deliciously bitter cranberries that add a very unique taste;

- Grains, such as rye, oat, buckwheat, barley – both whole (widely used in soups and gruels) and ground into flour. Flour is used not only in baking, as you might imagine, but also as a soup thickener;

- Pulses, like beans, peas, and lentils, also widely used in soups;

- Mushrooms in all forms, including powdered, dried, and pickled ones. And don't expect it to be champignons, because they aren't traditional at all – it has to be forest mushrooms. Pickled mushrooms and vegetables (as well as small pieces of salted meat or lard) are also traditionally used as snacks served with hard alcohol - vodka and nalivka, but that's a whole other topic;

- Dressings and spices, usually caraway, linseed, coriander, mustard, horseradish, juniper, cherry and oak leaves. The leaves, mostly birch or maple leaves, are also famous for being used as a baking paper replacement for baking true authentic bread in the oven.

Not to be dramatic, but traditional Belarusian bread is to die for. It's dark, heavy, and a little sour, made with rye flour, sometimes with additives like caraway seeds, sunflower seeds, or linseeds. Belarusians used a special kind of leaven instead of yeast, giving this bread a unique taste and a good texture.

Lots of people associate potatoes with Ireland, but that's just because they don't know much about Belarus. Potatoes take a special place in the local cuisine and culture and are also a big subject of jokes about the national stereotypes. Potatoes have been introduced to the diet of local citizens only in the 18th century, but because they are hearty and nutritious, and also easy to grow and cook, they have quickly formed the basis of many Belarusian dishes for the remaining hundreds of years. These dishes contain potatoes in various states – from the simple boiled and mashed potatoes to more complicated recipes. The famous draniki – thick potato pancakes, sometimes filled with minced meat (they are called kolduny, which literally translates as "warlocks"), are one of them. You can also try potato sausages, kletski – boiled balls of grated potatoes, or babka – potato casserole with bacon and onions.

Dairy products include butter, homemade cheese of cow and goat milk, and milk, in general, is a popular ingredient in various soups and gruels.

Belarusian cuisine also offers a huge variety of meat and poultry dishes made in a specific local manner. Some of the most famous are kumpyachok (salted and dried ham made of pork loin), machanka (a local version of meat gravy, usually served with pancakes or turned into a thick soup), and smazhanka (pastry with sausage, that resembles meat pies or very thick pizza). Homemade sausages and dishes made of meat co-products are also very popular, especially in the countryside.

14

The recipes of Belarusian villagers had to be fresh, hearty and easy to cook (although many of them had to be prepared in the oven for a long time on low heat), while the nobles could afford more exquisite recipes with more spices, a bigger variety of ingredients, and more sophisticated cooking technologies. The famous dishes of the rich were elk lips in sugared vinegar, rooster broth, and stuffed eels.

Belarusians have always worked hard and played hard. So, of course, local cuisine includes traditional desserts as well. Honey has been the main ingredient for desserts for many centuries: drinks and pastry were made out of it. Kulaga – thick gruel made of malt, flour, and berries – and simple baked apples were also very popular. The list of traditional desserts also has sweet pancakes and pears a la Radziwill (spiced and roasted in honey).

Drinks

The oldest alcoholic drinks of the Belarusians were based on beer and honey. Turning regular bee honey into drinkable one needs a technology that is similar to beer brewing. The wine wasn't a common drink since grapes were only grown on small vineyards belonging to the wealthiest families, and imported wines were also a luxury.

Traditionally, the most common drinks of Belarusian nobility were liquors, nalivkas, and nastoykas. The last two are strong and sweet alcoholic beverages based on vodka but enhanced with the flavors of berries, herbs, and/or honey. Today you can try those traditional drinks in restaurants and rural tourism estates, as well as buy them in regular stores and special retail outlets belonging to certain alcohol brands.

The most famous alcoholic drink in Belarus is probably vodka, also known there as garelka, or burnt wine, served on special occasions. It has been around since the 15th century and survived until today with enhanced recipes and in different versions. Modern liquor producers offer quite a big variety of vodkas, as well as nastoykas and balsams. Some of the options are bread vodka, cranberry vodka, vodka with pepper and honey, vodka with birch buds extract, balsams with herbs and fruits, and "zubrovka" – a classic bitter nastoyka with special herbs from Belovezhskaya Pushcha.

Belarusian beer breweries, or brovars, are producing delicious beers that combine traditional recipes and modern approach, and the quality of the drinks has been recognized at various international competitions. Mini-breweries with craft beer are extremely popular among the local youth. Alivaria, the oldest Belarusian brewery, was founded in 1864, and its main building has the Museum of Beer that you can visit. The tour will include old beer-making equipment, a huge collection of bottles and tags from different times, as well as learning about the current beer production process and beer tasting.

And now to non-alcoholic beverages!

Sbiten, a traditional Slavic hot drink that's best for winter, is based on honey or molasses mixed with spices, herbs, and sugar. Belarusian sbiten has its own features that make it a bit different from the recipes in other countries: it can include birch leaves, lime flowers, calamus, and for religious celebrations radish was added to the drink as well. You can find it on the menu at farmsteads and in restaurants that offer traditional Belarusian food. Lots of other traditional drinks were based on wild berries, birch, and maple. One of the popular homemade drinks today is compote, made of berries and fruits that are boiled in sugared water for a short amount of time. Kisel is another traditional drink that is basically thin drinkable jelly that is mostly made of various fruits and berries.

Belarusian kvas deserves a specific mention. Kvas is a cold drink (perfect for a hot summer day) made of naturally fermented bread or cereal – rye or barley. As strange as it sounds, it has a distinctive taste that reminds of dark beer. Bottled kvas is widely sold in grocery stores and supermarkets, and in summer you can also find street vendors that sell it on tap. Some kvas festivals occur in Belarus every year, featuring entertainment shows and kvas tasting. The biggest one is usually held in the city of Lida (Grodno region) where the huge beer and kvas production plant, famous all around the country, is located.

TRANSPORT IN BELARUS

GUEST CARDS FOR TOURISTS

If you have an intention to visit as many popular touristic places as you can in a short amount of time, a special guest card can be a really useful thing. It's a convenient smart-card that gives you discounts and bonuses at various touristic places and makes your stay in Belarus significantly easier. There are several different types of cards, some of which will grant you free transportation by public transport, as well as the free entrance in certain popular touristic locations. You can easily purchase a suitable card in several kiosks located in Minsk or online at minskpass.by, and the website will also offer you all of the necessary information about the card types. It would be a perfect option for those who will only stay in Minsk and its surroundings, but these cards can also help you get discounts on more than 200 places all around the country. So you can check the options at the website and find a perfect choice for your travel plans and needs.

The transportation system of Belarus is well-developed, so if you're planning a trip by yourself, without the help of a travel agency, it would be easy for you to plan your route and get anywhere you want by the most suitable way of transportation.

The first thing you might need to know is **how to get to Minsk from the Minsk National Airport**. There are a few ways of doing it.

The cheapest one is to go by the regular-route bus number 300Э that looks like a city bus. It circulates between the city and the airport around the clock, but less frequently at night. The bus will take you straight to the central bus station in Minsk, next door to the central railway station (which would be convenient in case Minsk isn't your final destination), and it also has several stops near subway stations on its way. You can purchase tickets either via the special terminal inside the airport or directly from the bus driver, as well as online. The bus stop is located right in front of the Gate 5-6 on the ground floor of the airport building.

Shuttle buses number 1400-TK and 1430-TK, which you can find at the same bus stop, are a little faster, but operate less frequently, and hold a smaller quantity of passengers. 1400-TK will take you to the central bus station in Minsk. 1430-TK has the same final destination, but it will also make a stop near the Mogilevskaya metro station. You can buy tickets online, via the terminal, or from the driver as well.

The bus number 173Э operates several times a day, and it will take you to the Sokol micro-district. Its stop can be found in front of the Gate 5-6 on the ground floor as well. You can get to the Mogilevskaya metro station from Sokol as well.

Car rent is both convenient and reliable for those who plan their trips on their own and prefer to depend only on their personal schedules. If that's the option that you need, you can contact one of these services with good reviews:

- Sixt http://www.sixt.by/en/, phone: +375296044482;

- Europcar https://europcar.by/, phone: +375291336553;

- Interrent https://www.interrent.com/car-hire/belarus/minsk/minsk-airport, phone: +375172792241.

Other trusted car rental services' booths can be found at the ground floor of the airport building, located near the arrival gates so that you won't miss them.

Another way to reach your destination from the Minsk Airport is to hire a taxi or an Uber from the airport via an app, by phone, or by catching a taxi straight at the entrance. It's probably the most expensive option, as it always is with taxis, but it would be especially convenient if you arrive late at night when the public transport in Minsk isn't working. You can also hire a taxi from the central bus station. Some of the most popular apps for taxi services are NextApp, Taxi 135, Yandex Taxi (it works not only in Minsk, but all over the country as well), and, of course, UberBY.

If you're organizing a trip for someone important or a group of people, you can hire a special transfer vehicle online at https://airport.by/en/transport/transfer-hr or in the transfer pavilions inside the airport (near the arrival sectors 3-4 and 5-6). They also offer document delivery services.

Urban transport is widespread throughout Minsk and other localities. Buses operate in almost all towns and cities all around the country except for the smallest ones, trolleybuses exist in the biggest cities, trams operate in Minsk, Vitebsk, Mozyr, and Novopolotsk, and the only metro in the country operates in Minsk.

Unlike many European cities, the metro is located completely below the ground, and it doesn't extend beyond the city limits. New stations are added quite often to fit the needs of the constantly growing and expanding city, but the scheme and the train direction system isn't hard for understanding at all. Every metro station is a masterpiece of its own, both Soviet-style and newly built ones, so you can spend some time getting off the train on each station to see their design. Taking pictures very openly in the subway is forbidden, but there's a very low chance that a smartphone would be too noticeable. You won't receive any penalty for doing it. Another thing to mention about the metro are the checkpoints at the entrance. The policemen often check huge bags and instrument cases for safety matters, but it absolutely doesn't mean that using the metro is dangerous.

Buses, trolleybuses and trams' numeration system is pretty complicated and illogical, so downloading a transport app (like Goes, MinskRoutes, Yandex Transport, or Moovit) or using the information at http://www.minsktrans.by/en/ would make it much easier. A lot of busy transport stops in Minsk feature electronic scoreboards with the transport schedule in Russian and English.

Transport tickets can be purchased in vending kiosks at the stops, in the metro ticket office, from the bus, trolleybus, or tram driver (cash only, and not more than 5 rubles), or from the conductor, if they're present inside the vehicle. There are no conductors in Minsk, but there are electronic validators in every vehicle instead. You can also purchase transport cards for certain transport types, that will save you from stuffing paper tickets or metro tokens in all of your pockets. The cards either have unlimited usage of said transport for a certain amount of days or a certain number of rides. You can easily refill the card in any ticket office.

Automobile transport, buses and minibuses in particular, is, probably, the most popular way of traveling around the country. There are regular bus routes organized all over the place, the tickets can be purchased easily, and all of the schedules are available online. Atlas and Busfor are quite useful apps for all sorts of bus tickets, including international ones. Unfortunately, both apps only have the Russian language, but it's still possible to use them since they're not too complicated. Eurolines and Ecolines buses are also highly popular among travelers. You can check out https://new.ticketbus.by/en_US/shop online booking system as well.

Railway transport in Belarus can be used both for long-distance rides and as a local equivalent for European city rails. New and convenient "city line" trains only go to the close suburbs of Minsk, but they have the full vibe of European trains.

In general, Belarus has several types of train transportation for passengers. Urban lines operate within the main city of the district and to the stations in the satellite towns; regional work within one region; interregional lines connect the main cities of the Belarusian districts; international lines go abroad and beyond. There's also a choice between business and economy class, but the difference doesn't depend entirely on the seat types and services offered. It also depends on the train speed and the number of stops on their way. The cheapest ones stop on every little whistle-stop, and it can take quite a while.

The tickets can be bought at the ticket offices on the railway stations, some of them are also available online. You can also check https://rasp.rw.by/en/ for the train schedules, and https://www.rw.by/en/ would be a really useful resource for you to book and purchase your train tickets – to find out which ones can be booked and what features would your particular train have. There also are transport cards for those who use suburban trains very often, so if that's your plan, you can purchase a card like this in any railway ticket office.

Air transport for tourists does not exist inside Belarus since the country is relatively small. The Minsk National Airport, as it was mentioned above, welcomes international flights. The airports in the district capital cities work with charter flights, cargo airships, and offer emergency landings. Gomel, Grodno, and Brest airports also offer regular flights to Kaliningrad, the city belonging to Russia.

Water transport in Belarus is represented by ten river ports. The demand for passenger transportation by water bodies is quite low, but water sightseeing tours are a highly popular tourist attraction during the warm seasons. These tours are organized in the following places:

- Vitebsk, by the Zapadnaya Dvina river;

- Grodno and its nearby surroundings, by Neman river and the Augustow Canal (the Augustow Canal also offers short tours on board of a water bus);

- Brest, by the Mukhavets river;

- Gomel, by the Sozh river;

- Bobruisk, by the Berezina river;

- Mogilev, by the Dnepr river;

- Pinsk and Mozyr, by the Pripyat river;

- The Pripyatsky national park and its water bodies;

- The national park Narochansky, by the very famous Naroch Lake;

- The national park Braslavskiye Ozera, by the Drivyaty lake;

- By Zaslavl water reservoir near Minsk, also widely known among the locals as Minsk Sea;

- By the Vygonoshchanskoye lake.

CASTLES OF BELARUS

THANKS TO ITS LONG HISTORY, BELARUS AND ITS TERRITORY LIVED through a lot of events, and lots of influential and wealthy families have built their posh manors on the picturesque lands of the country. So, Belarusian castles can be divided into two categories: the ancient ones that were built for military purposes in the Middle Ages, and luxurious manors that were built later in time and were not supposed to be military fortifications. Even though some castles from the second category had the necessary safety measures, they, unlike the medieval ones, were very focused on the beautiful exterior and interior design and the comfort of the living space of their founders and the founders' guests and families. Despite the fact that Belarusian architecture suffered a lot because of various armed conflicts on the territory of the country, there are quite many castles that are decently preserved to these days or purposefully restored, and will definitely be interesting for visiting.

The Mir Castle in Grodno region is, probably, the most famous Belarusian castle ever. You will find the pictures of this gothic-style building on postcards, magnets, mugs, every possible piece of merchandise, in articles about Belarus, on book covers, you name it. You might have noticed that the castle looks a little strange – as if two different pieces were glued together. That's because it was originally meant to be a fort in the 16th century, but after the castle got into the hands of the Radziwill family, they made adjustments to the plan, and the building was finished in a different style to serve as a spacious castle meant for living. After the Soviet Union was formed, the castle was used for several different purposes, which resulted in the damaging of its interior, but now it's mostly restored and ready for the tours.

There are ghost stories and other legends that surround this castle, and they are officially told during the tours. So, if you're curious about mystical old castles, you should definitely go and check this one out! Currently, the castle is a very touristic place that can endure a huge stream of people. It hosts a lot of events, can be rented for weddings, has a hotel, a restaurant that cooks authentic dishes, and a conference hall inside. You can book a tour of the castle or read about the events at https://mirzamak.by/en/.

A curious fact is that the word "mir" – the name of the town where the castle is – means "peace" in Belarusian, and both "peace" and "world" in Russian.

The Nesvizh Castle in Minsk region is the second famous castle. There are no official "castle fame" ratings, but this castle goes in pair with the Mir castle whenever the first one is mentioned. Both of these castles belonged to the Radziwill family, and the legend said that the underground tunnel for the carriages was connecting these two castles, but it was never proven to be true despite the researches with modern technologies. The Nesvizh castle is also highly popular among tourists and has a huge amount of people coming to see it throughout the year. The official website of the castle is https://niasvizh.by/en/.

Due to political reasons, this castle changed the owners several times, was turned into a sanatorium in Soviet times, and most of its original atmosphere and interior was lost. However, it underwent the complicated restoration process, and its current furnishing, though not entirely consisting of the antique furniture, replicates the castle's best times pretty similarly. The castle is surrounded by many legends, and some of them are even reenacted during the castle tours. You can also visit the Catholic church with the Radziwill family tombs, which is located not too far from the castle itself.

The Lida Castle in Grodno region is the oldest preserved castle on the territory of Belarus, its construction being completed in 1328. It has served its purpose of being a military fortification, and it's considered to be built in a similar way that the castles in Northern Europe were made. The castle may seem very simple and boring at first, but even if you're visiting it not during one of the medieval historical reconstruction festivals, there would be something to see, or you can just look at it, being fascinated by how old the building is. Inside the castle, there is a museum that showcases the life of the castle's inhabitants and old weapons of these times. One of the castle's walls, the south one, still has the original lancet holes of the 14th century.

The Kossovo Castle, located in the Brest region, is also called **the**

Puslovsky castle since it originally belonged to the Puslovsky family when it was built in the 1840s. However, not for long, because the castle's founder's son was an irresponsible person who had gambling issues, and one day he just lost the castle because of his debts. The legend goes that the castle is now inhabited by the ghost of Countess Puslovskaya, the castle founder's wife who was infuriated by the fact that her son lost their family manor in a card game. But she will reveal herself only if you misbehave on the territory of the castle, so don't worry about that.

Since then, the castle has changed many owners and suffered during wars and fire. But from 2008 til 2017 it underwent the serious renovations, and currently, everyone can enjoy this amazing place made in an absolutely unique for Belarus architectural style and its gorgeous interiors. People say that the twelve towers represent the twelve months of the year, and the central four, the tallest ones, are symbolizing the harvest months. There's also a hotel and a restaurant on the territory.

The castle in Krevo, Grodno region, was a significant place for the history of the Grand Duchy of Lithuania because this is the exact place where the Krevo Act which united Lithuania and Poland was signed. The castle hasn't survived until the present days, but the ruins of it look quite impressive. There was a legend that underneath the castle was a tunnel that was going straight to Vilnius, the capital city of Lithuania. The castle in Medininkai, Lithuania, is considered the exact (but preserved) copy of the Krevo castle, that was built at the same time and was a part of the same fortification frontier. Many tournaments and other folklore events are now held among the ruins of Krevo castle.

. . .

The Ruzhany castle in the Brest region was one of the largest castle complexes on the territory of Belarus. It belonged to the Sapega family – some of the most influential people in Belarusian history. It was originally built as a fort but later rebuilt to become a beautiful living palace with a church, a monastery, and a tavern. Unfortunately, after the huge fire in 1914 and the attempts of reconstruction, the castle was eventually destroyed during World War II. The restoration process is currently happening, and some parts of the castle are open to the public and have a museum dedicated to the Sapega family inside. The picture of this castle can be found on several Belarusian postal stamps of 2017. The castle's website is http://ruzhany.museum.by/en.

The underground tunnel legends were really popular among people back then, so Ruzhany castle also had one. It was believed that this castle and the Kossovo one, that is located only 25 km away, were connected with a large tunnel for carriages. Why? Who knows.

The Lyubcha castle, Grodno region, is considered to be a lesser-known one, but its beauty is hard to underestimate. It stands on the bank of the Neman River in the incredibly picturesque location. The construction process began in the 16th century, and it was a wooden castle, but later became a stone one. It was completely destroyed and rebuilt several times throughout its history. What was left of it eventually was just a couple of towers.

Currently, the Lyubcha castle is being restored, but this isn't paid out of the government's budget. It is done fully with the help of volunteers and sponsors. Their website is http://lubcza.by/, which is, unfortunately, only in Russian, but the castle is open for tourists and hosts various events, so, if you'll want to help, it's possible to find out, how. The Lyubcha castle is the only castle in the world that is being restored only by volunteers.

The New and Old Castles in Grodno, despite standing near one another, weren't built at the same time by the same people at all. They have entirely different, yet connected, histories, but are both absolutely worth visiting.

The Old Castle, the way it's seen now, was slowly constructed in the 14th century on the remains of an even more ancient castle of the Black Ruthenian rulers of the 11th century. It was owned by several well-known governors, such as Vytautas the Great, Casimir IV Jagiellon, and Stephen Bathory. It was damaged in several wars, and after the Great Northern War, the damage was so extensive that its inhabitants had to move into the New Castle. After that, the Old Castle was rebuilt and simplified, given to the military department of the Russian Empire, and turned into a museum in 1924.

The New Castle, built as King August III's property, played an important role in the history of the Rzecz Pospolita, as the document that declared its breakup was sighed here by the said king's successor, King Stanislaw II Augustus, in 1795. After that, the building was used as cadets' corps, then as a war hospital, later it suffered in World War II and after that used as an administrative office. Since 1991 it functions as a museum and gallery.

. . .

The castle of Golshany, Grodno region, isn't too well-preserved. In fact, there currently are just ruins of this previously magnificent place with a sad history. There are many legends and tragic stories tied to the existence of this castle, that even are represented in literature. The thing is – the castle was built by Pawel Stefan Sapega, a member of a very wealthy and influential family in the history of the Grand Duchy of Lithuania, but after his death, no one cared about the castle anymore. It was slowly deteriorating, sold and resold to several different owners, and World War II destroyed it completely. Local people, trying to rebuild the town after the war, disassembled the castle even further, building the House of Culture and a pigpen out of its bricks. However, the remnants of the castle still radiate glory, and annual Middle Ages festivals are held near its walls.

Another thing about this castle is that it's believed that you can encounter one of the two local ghosts there. The Black Monk is believed to be the soul of a young poor man who was killed for the crime of loving the young Duchess of Golshany. Another ghost, the White Lady, is a young woman who was sacrificed because of the difficulties during the construction of the important church near the castle. The Middle Ages were truly violent times, but don't let that ruin your impression of these magnificent castle ruins that survived through history and inspired many people.

Gatovsky-Poklevsky-Kozel castle (the Krasny Bereg manor) in the Gomel region is a place that not too many foreign tourists know of, yet it's surprisingly well-preserved and open for guided tours and independent exploration. It was built at the end of the 19th century in the mix of architectural styles from gothic to modern, and some specialists say that there also are Arabic motifs in the building's look. In 2015 the manor was fully restored to be a museum and opened for the general public. Its thoroughly restored interior will take you back in time to tell you a story of this manor the way it was before the Russian Revolution. A reason why the building has been preserved so well and wasn't left in ruins is that during World War II it was chosen to serve as a hospital and a children's expulsion camp by the German army, and later used as a hospital by the USSR army. A memorial dedicated to these dark times is located in a place that is not far from the manor. On the territory of this castle, you can also visit the slightly abandoned garden and make a wish at the old mysterious stone with two triangular holes.

The Rumyantsev-Paskevich Residence, or, simply, **the Gomel Palace**, is another place of historical importance in the Gomel region. It stands on the bank of the Sozh River, surrounded by a romantic scenic park, which is a masterpiece of the park design itself. The residence includes not just the palace itself, but also the chapel with the family tombs, the neoclassical church of Saints Peter and Paul, and several subsidiary buildings. You can book a tour inside the castle, and even though the original building was taken from the owners by the USSR government, severely damaged in several armed conflicts, and restored later, its exposition is impressively large, and the interior is as historically accurate as it could be executed. The castle's original owners were the influential family of militarists and politicians of the Russian state, so this building has seen a lot, and the tour would give you an impression of what the life of the influential people looked like in the 19th century.

NATURE OF BELARUS

THE CHERNOBYL DISASTER OF 1986 HAS INFLUENCED THE LOCAL nature, especially the Gomel region, therefore you might have some concerns about this situation. However, it's scientifically approved that currently, the health risk for the visitors of the country is minimal. The most contaminated areas are strictly controlled and you won't be able to visit them without the approval of the officials.

93 percent of the country's territory is covered with natural vegetation, and one-third of it all is the forest. Local forests are incredibly rich in their species, both flora, and fauna. Natural lakes are spread all over Belarus, but especially many of them are located in the north of the country. The rich diversity of local wildlife, including the rare species reflected in the Red Book, is protected in numerous wildlife reserves, sanctuaries, and other conservation projects. There are five National Parks all across Belarus, protected by the government and supported by UNESCO. Each one of them can be visited, and this kind of pastime totally won't leave you disappointed.

Belavezhskaya Pushcha in the Brest region is the most famous national park since it was declared the World Heritage Site. It's home to a large number of ancient oak trees over 500 years old, as well as many species of animals and birds. The world's largest population of very rare European bison lives there. You can see them and several other rare local species at the zoo right in the Pushcha, or you can take one of the many hiking trails to enjoy the undisturbed nature. It would be the best option to visit the park as a part of an organized tour since you'll need to have a special permit to park your own vehicle there. You can stay in any of the hotels or at the farm tourist estates. In winter, special tours for kids are wildly popular since Belovezhskaya Pushcha hosts the residence of Father Frost – the local version of Santa Klaus. The park's official website is https://npbp.by/eng/.

Berezinsky Biosphere Reserve lies in the Vitebsk region and represents the unique cohabitation and synergy of forests, water bodies, meadows, and bogs. More than half of all known species of Belarusian flora and fauna coexist there on 85 thousand hectares, some of these species listed in the Red Book. If you decide to go there, don't forget your camera and binoculars, because you'll have the possibility to observe this beauty from a 15m watchtower. The forest also owns a zoo, where you can take a closer look at some of the species. Other things you can do while uniting with nature is taking a walk along one of the eco-trails, ride a horse, hang out at the rope playground (pun intended), and rent a canoe or a bicycle. The park employees offer naturalistic studies for kids. You can find all the information at www.berezinsky.by/en/.

The Naroch National Park in the Minsk region is named after and mostly dedicated to, the largest lake in Belarus – Lake Naroch. What will you find there? Incredibly scenting pine forests, a giant variety of plant species, including the rare ones, three groups of lakes and numerous streams of natural mineral water, and a very popular among the locals and the tourists wellness resort with over ten sanatoriums and health centers built all around the territory of the national park. You can involve yourself in hiking, sailing, helicopter trips in the summer, hunting, or fishing – Lake Naroch is an absolute fisherman's dream.

The Pripyat National Park, located in the south of Belarus in the Polesie lowlands, is spread on both sides of the Pripyat River and includes high wetlands and great preservation of natural complexes. The park has preserved the monuments of historical inhabitants of Polesie territory. You can also visit the Nature Museum to get acquainted with the cultural, historical, and archaeological heritage. Moreover, being a national park, Pripyat offers you its breathtaking landscapes of the flood plains, walks along its eco-trails to the "king oak" and the "king pine", and a sailing tour on the Pripyat River.

Braslavskie Ozera (the Lakes of Braslav) National Park in the Vitebsk region is a unique gem in the crown of Belarusian nature. It includes rare species, untouched forests, wetlands, numerous lakes, monuments of culture, nature, and history. Among them are glacial landforms, boulders, lake islands, ancient settlements, and their burial grounds – all of that attract hikers and travelers all around the world. The park will offer you fishing, hunting, water recreation, and just walking along the trails enjoying all the beauty of nature. International fishing tournaments are actually held there. In the center of the park, you'll find the ancient town of Braslav, which happens to be the research center of the park, and you can book a tour to go there. The official website of the park is https://braslavpark.by/en/.

Best camping sites

Camping is a rather cheap way to spend your holiday with a good view and being close to nature. Belarus offers you a variety of outdoor recreation, and camping is appreciated by the visitors of the country due to its availability. You can rent a tent-place and the tent itself, or camp on wheels. Some places allow fishing for a certain price with the limited weight of fishing per day for one fisherperson.

The territory of **Braslav Lakes National Park** in the Vitebsk region would be an incredible option for those who love lake views and prefer them over the forests. There are more than five touristic camps organized there, with no pre-booking necessary, however, if you want to go fishing there, you'll need to purchase a fishing permit in advance (https://braslavpark.by/en/rybalka/). The camping sites are equipped with toilets, garbage bins, and specifically marked safe spots for fireplaces. S'mores are definitely coming to your mind right now, but, so that you know, they aren't really a thing in the local culture, even though no one would stop you from making them. When it comes to traditional camping food, local people usually boil fish soup on an open fire (ideally it is a fish soup, but sometimes just instant noodles), bake potatoes in the embers, and make grilled meat using skewers. The last dish is also known as shashlik and is similar to kebab or barbecue.

The **Duby** ("Oaks" in Russian") **camping site** in Grodno region is a calm place on the Novoye lake not far from the shore of the mesmerizing Neman river. You can rent a guest house, a tent, or a place to bring your own tent. You'll be able to use a shared kitchen at the property and sauna in any case. The Novoye lake is amazing for fishing and swimming, and in between these activities, you can take a walk in the forest among the relic oaks.

The **car camping place "Naroch"** in the Minsk region is located on the shore of the largest Belarusian lake Naroch, and it will surprise you with the gorgeous pine forest around it, the clear water, and the beautiful shore. Swimming in Lake Naroch is not allowed, but lots of other activities are easily available – windsurfing, kiting, sports and active games. The camping site is located near the Naroch resort village where you can buy food or simply go for a stroll. You can stay in a hotel, book a bungalow, or set up a tent, and there is not only the parking space for regular cars but motorhomes as well.

30 km away from Naroch you can find the **"Blue Lakes" natural complex** that is worth visiting as well. There you can hike up an eco-trail for a small fee, swim in a couple of lakes where it's allowed, and have a break from the haste and information overload, since the cell phone signal is really poor in this area. Don't worry, the information signs won't leave you hanging. You can stay overnight at a touristic farmstead or bring your own tent.

If you are looking for a specific local atmosphere, you can pay a visit to **the village-museum-ethnographic complex named Zabrodye** in the Minsk region. Unfortunately, their website only has the Russian language, but you can contact them via phone, Viber, or email (https://zabrodje.com/contacts.php). It's a unique place that is often used as a filming location, it offers several differently furnished (according to different times) places to stay, as well as the camping site, it has several museums on its territory, saunas, homemade food, retro vehicle driving, gazebos, and more.

Religious tourism

Belarus is a country of many cultures, located at the crossroads of faiths and denominations, and you will encounter numerous churches, cathedrals, convents, and monasteries – ancient and new. Most religious buildings don't allow regular tourists in, and you can get there only if you are a member of the certain religious community and your purpose of going there is based on your faith. But some of them serve as both touristic attractions and functional churches at the same time, especially the ones that are considered historical monuments. Pilgrims and tourists come to Belarus from all around the world to admire the magnificent architecture and impressive history that goes way back, and to attend religious festivals and celebrations.

Some of the local temples were nominated for the UNESCO World Heritage List. For many centuries, many different religions and architectural styles have been intertwining on the Belarusian territory to eventually form a unique cocktail of architectural styles and buildings that you see now. You most likely won't be able to find this anywhere else in the world. The churches listed here are the most well-known and notable, and definitely worth visiting for touristic purposes, even if you're not into religion.

The biggest two categories are Orthodox and Roman Catholic churches. Mosques and synagogues are present too, as well as several temples of less "popular" faiths. The only **museum of religion** in Belarus is located in Grodno, and its exposition is dedicated to the archaic beliefs of local people, Christianity, Judaism, and Islam. The building of the museum is a former palace that was built in Classicism and Baroque architectural styles in the 18th-19th centuries.

ORTHODOX CHURCHES

THE ANCIENT TOWN OF POLOTSK, VITEBSK REGION, IS THE MOST famous attraction for those who are interested in Orthodox faith and their churches. The history of Polotsk and its leaders is closely intertwined with the history of Orthodox faith in the territory of Belarus. St. Euphrosyne, the holy patroness of Belarus, founded **the Convent of Our Savior and St. Euphrosyne** in her hometown Polotsk. This town is also home to one of Belarus' most ancient and well-known churches – the **Holy Transfiguration Church**, the walls of which are decorated with unique frescos that date back to the 12th century. The relics of St. Euphrosyne and the copy of the widely known St. Euphrosyne Cross, one of the Belarusian sacred objects, that is, unfortunately, lost, are kept there. You can see the picture of this sacred cross and the Holy Transfiguration Church on the 10-ruble banknote.

Another true architectural and religious gem of Polotsk is the famous **St. Sophia Cathedral**, which was built in the 11th century, becoming the very first stone temple on the territory of Belarus. The similar churches dedicated to St. Sophia are located in Kiev, Ukraine and Novgorod, Russia. The walls of the church were previously decorated with murals, however, currently, there are only fragments of them that are left. Today this cathedral is a part of Polotsk History and Culture Museum, where you can find out all about its history and architecture (and it has been rebuilt and readjusted numerous times). You can find the Boris Stone –one of the four of them that survived to the present day. It's a large stone with crosses and inscriptions, named after the Duke Boris Vseslavovich, who ruled the land in the 12th century.

The town of Turov, located in the Gomel region, is the second oldest religious and spiritual center of Belarus after Polotsk. The **All Saints Church** that stands there isn't extremely old, it was built in 1801 as a regular local church. But what makes it remarkable is that it stands near the remains of the 12th-century Christian cemetery. Another famous attraction of Turov is the stone crosses, that, according to the legend, have sailed on the river waters all the way from Kiev, where the Christianization of Kievan Rus' had happened at the end of the 10th century. Only three of these crosses have survived to the present day. Another stone cross is believed to be growing straight out of the ground for the last 20 years, and this place is considered to be sacred as well.

The oldest functioning church in Belarus is the **Saints Boris and Gleb Church**, also known as **Kolozhskaya Church**. It's located on a steep riverbank of the Neman River in Grodno, which did a really bad job to the building throughout the centuries. It was built around 1140-1170, using the technology that was unique back then: there were clay pots sealed inside its walls to help with the distribution of the sound inside of the church. It was designed following the **traditions of the Byzantine temple architecture**, yet it has no direct analogs neither in the Old Russian nor in the Balkan architecture. Its walls are

39

decorated with polished stones and multicolor cross-shaped majolica tiles, which is also a unique feature. However, no matter how amazing and progressive the church was, the riverbed, changing over time, made it slowly fall apart, and now there's only a half of the original building left, the other half renovated in a completely different style with an intention not to mimic the old one.

The first thing you'll see upon arrival to the village of Sarya, Vitebsk region, is the beautiful neo-gothic **church of the Holy Assumption of Saint Virgin Mary**. Traditionally, churches in this style are associated with the Catholic faith, and this one was originally meant to serve as a catholic church, but due to the bureaucratic complications and political situation around the time of its construction, it was given to the Orthodox diocese. It still remains an Orthodox church to these days.

The Holy Resurrection Cathedral in Borisov, Minsk region, is a monument of pseudo-Russian architectural style, that was built in 1874. Before that, there was a wooden church in its place that was rebuilt several times due to war and, later, fire. Near the church, you'll find a monument dedicated to Duke Boris Vseslavich – the founder of Borisov.

Zditovo village, in Brest region, is home to one of the oldest churches - **the church of St. Nikita**, originally built in 1502 in the Western-Polesian style. It was rebuilt several times but has remained its laconic exterior, typical for the Orthodox churches in the villages. It was a functioning church since its very opening, even during the times of religious persecution, and it has never been damaged neither during wars nor due to natural disasters of any sort.

The Holy Assumption Cathedral in Vitebsk is a unique building not only because it's located in an unbelievably picturesque place, but also because it currently is the only cathedral in Vitebsk with its lower functioning floor located under the ground. The church was built in the place of a former pagan sanctuary of the 12th century, destroyed, rebuilt, and destroyed many times. The first wooden "version" of this cathedral was built there in 1406, and the current building was opened in 2011.

CATHOLIC CHURCHES

St. Francis Xavier Cathedral in the very center of Grodno can be seen from far away in any weather. Its bright white building is constructed in baroque style, and originally it was a Jesuit church, however, in 1991 it became a cathedral after the new diocese was built in Grodno. Just like every major church in Belarus, it was not functioning as a religious building during the USSR times but was re-established in the late 1980s. The colors of the cathedral look minimalistic on the outside, but the inside of it looks absolutely stunning, rich with statues, frescoes, and pillars. One of the cathedral's towers has Europe's oldest clocks on it.

The Trinity Church in the agro town of Gervyaty, Grodno region, is an outstanding piece of architecture located in a very scenic place. Before it, there was a wooden church in the same place, built in 1526, but on the verge of the 19th century, it was replaced by a stone neo-gothic building built by a famous Polish and Lithuanian architect Vatslav Mikhnevich. People often call it "little Switzerland" and "Notre

Dame of Belarus". In front of the Trinity church, you'll see several wooden crosses decorated with carvings, which is very typical for Lithuanian churches.

St. Anna Church in Mosar, in the Vitebsk region, is an incredibly famous place for religious tourism. This temple doesn't only include the old and beautiful church, a monument of classicism, there are also several other landmarks on its grounds. The chapel where the Icon of Our Lady of the Gate of Dawn is kept, a bell tower, ancient gate, a large park with artificial ponds, sculptures, the biggest Catholic cross in Belarus, the remains of St. Justinian, an ostrich farm, the natural spring of holy water, and other remarkable things. The history of this village is inspiring: priest Juozas Bulka led the restoration of this church and inspired the villagers to stop drowning their lives in alcohol. Now Mosar is a zone of total sobriety and a well-known pilgrimage destination.

The Bernardine Church of the Assumption of the Blessed Virgin Mary in Budslav, Minsk region, is the largest Catholic temple of Belarus, and it holds the Budslav Icon of Our Lady, that was proclaimed to be the patron icon of Belarus. This church was mentioned for the first time in 1504, but in 1783 it was completed in the way that we see it today. It played a large role in the local community and served as a school, a hospital, and a house for the monks and priests. During World War II, the front line passed directly through Budslav three times, but the church wasn't damaged at all. One of the remarkable features of this church is its ancient organ, made in the 18th century.

. . .

The Church of the Nativity of the Blessed Virgin Mary (the Trinity Church) in Vidzy, Vitebsk region, is the second-largest Catholic church in Belarus after the one in Budslav. It was built in 1914, badly damaged in World War I, then suffered from World War II and during the Soviet times, when it was used as a gym and grain storage. It was returned to the Catholic church and restored in 1989. This beautiful tall building is made of red brick in the neo-gothic style – a typical thing for Catholic churches. You will definitely enjoy looking at its soaring shapes and stained-glass windows.

Church of Saints Simeon and Helena, also known as **the Red Church**, located in Minsk, is a fully functioning church that hosts a lot of events, including organ music concerts, and a huge touristic attraction at the same time. People are allowed to come inside even during the church service if they'll be quiet. It looks stunning both from the inside and from the outside thanks to its architectural style and beautiful stained-glass windows. This church had a long history since its opening in 1910, being secularized and used as a cinema when the USSR was formed, then used as a church by the German occupiers, then as a cinema again. Yet, in 1990 it was restored to function as a Catholic church.

Cathedral of the Holy Name of Mary in Minsk is located across the road from the City Hall, surrounded by other buildings. It was constructed in 1710 under the Polish rule for the Jesuit order, survived a few changes of governments, went through heavy fire and the intentional destruction by the Soviet government. It was given back to the Catholic church in 1993, fully renewed in 1997, and currently has an organ made in Austria and the restored frescos of the 18th century.

. . .

A very curious location is the **Kalvaryyskoye cemetery**. It's the oldest cemetery in Minsk, and it has an amazing neo-gothic chapel, that used to be Minsk's only functioning Catholic church during USSR times when religion was strictly banned at first and strongly disapproved of later. Even though it was closed from the late 1930s until the year 1980, it still counts as the only functional Catholic church in the whole city. Currently, this chapel is used for general worship, and the cemetery is home to the graves of several famous Belarusian and Polish people from the 19th century, as well as many soldiers' graves and the graves of the Jewish people from the Minsk Ghetto. You can find a monument dedicated to the victims of the Ghetto near the back entrance of the cemetery.

There's only one functioning **Protestant Church** in Belarus, that is located in Grodno. The town of Vetka in the Gomel region has a place for the **Old Believers**, as well as a large ethnographic museum of Old Beliefs and Belarusian Traditions. **The Great Synagogue of Grodno** is the oldest functional synagogue of Europe, being located in a very beautiful building constructed in 1578 that also has a museum of Jewish history inside of it. There also are several synagogues that are currently in the process of restoration. The town of Ivye in Grodno region has a huge population of Tatars, and there was the only functioning **mosque** there during the Soviet time. At the present time another mosque has been built in Minsk.

WAR HISTORY TOURISM

WAR AND MILITARY HISTORY TAKES A BIG PLACE IN BELARUSIANS'
minds. The last war was over more than 70 years ago, ending with the
victory of the USSR and enormous human casualties on both sides, yet
the celebrations and military parades are held every year on Victory
Day (the victory in the Great Patriotic War), May the 9th. Belarus also
celebrates Independence Day on the 3rd of July, which is basically the
anniversary of Belarusian land being freed from the fascist occupation –
a more local Victory Day. This is a thing that may seem really strange
to a foreigner, because a lot of Belarusians take their kids to the
celebrations and various themed reenactments, dressing them up in
soldiers' uniforms; and the aspects of war history, as well as war-
themed literature, are thoroughly studied in schools. Even though now
the number of people who went through this war, unfortunately, but
irreversibly, decreases every year, Belarusians believe that if this war
would be remembered (and heard of) by everyone, then a nightmare
like this would never happen again. The statement is questionable, and
many young people disagree with this position and disapprove of the
expensive and grotesque military parades, yet for now, it is the way it
is. Belarus is home to many important monuments of war history,

especially World War II, and they are taken good care of. Each one of them is hard to look at, for many reasons, but they were created by talented people and will definitely touch your heart and tell you the stories of the people who we lost.

The Bobruisk Fortress in the Mogilev region is considered to be the "elder sister" of the Brest Fortress. It had witnessed the War of 1812, the Decembrist revolt, and World War II, specifically the Eastern European Front of it, known as the Great Patriotic War. It was built to be a defense fort, and it also served as a prison for some time. The legend is that there was a special chamber inside of it, shaped like an egg, that makes the prisoner inside of it lose their mind in a couple of days. The Nazi army turned it into a concentration camp, and later it was used as a military warehouse and barracks. As every old place with messed up history, it's quite popular among tourists, open for tours, movie shootings, and archaeological studies.

The memorial complex in the village of Lesnaya in the Mogilev region is dedicated to the legendary battle that was a turning point for the Russian army during the Great Northern War in 1708. The complex includes a monument in the form of an eagle, the chapel of Apostle Peter, and a marble obelisk over the soldiers' common grave.

The Brest Fortress is the most famous citadel of Belarus. Despite its beauty, it's a very sad place that's dedicated to the memory of Belarusian soldiers who sacrificed their lives at the very beginning of the Great Patriotic War, holding off the Nazi army for 28 days, even though it was estimated that the fortress will fall very soon. The damaged

47

fortress is a unique architectural ensemble that tells a tragic story, and it consists of several parts, squares, and memorials, as well as the White Palace – one of the oldest stone buildings of the old Brest-Litovsk. The tours around the fortress are available throughout the day. For more information, you can contact brest-fortress@yandex.ru or +375162200365.

Stalin Line in Minsk region is the historical and cultural complex made out of the actual defense system created at the beginning of the 1930s. It's not a memorial, but more of an entertainment place. It organizes events and historical reenactments, you can visit an exposition, climb inside a real tank, drive an ATV, take a guided tour, and interact with actual weapons and other objects. People often take their children there, so, if it's your jam, you can do that as well. The website of the complex is https://stalin-line.by/en/.

The Grodno region is filled with **old machine gun nests**, used in the Great Patriotic War. They were a part of the Molotov Line, a fortified area on the USSR border that was created after Baltic countries joined the Union. The project wasn't completed in time before the war started, and the fortification did not serve its full purpose, however, the machine gun nests still played a big role in the defense of the country. Several of them are included in the official tours, while some can just be found on a map and visited by car. It's not allowed and not safe to climb inside of them, since they are very old and most of them were blown up and have cracks all over, but these abandoned pieces of concrete, covered with growing plants and slowly consumed by nature, are still very fascinating to look at, especially if you love war history.

. . .

The Khatyn memorial in the Minsk region is probably one of the most tragic places one could ever visit in their lifetime. It's dedicated to the tragedy that occurred in March of 1943, when an entire village of Khatyn, all of its villagers, were forced into a big shed that was then set on fire. The Nazis did that as a revenge act after several of their soldiers were killed by the locals. Only a few villagers managed to survive, either because they miraculously fled the burning shed or because they hid and stayed unnoticed. Khatyn commemorates not only its villagers but all of the lives of the Belarusians that were lost in this war. The website of the memorial complex is http://khatyn.by/en/. It hasn't been updated in a long time, but it still contains information about the tragic events, a map, and a virtual tour around the place.

Death camps and ghettos were spread all around Belarus due to the genocide policy of the Nazis. Several of them, like Ozarichi, Trostenets, and Minsk ghetto, are now turned into the memorials of those horrific times. The memorial named "Yama" ("the pit" in Russian and Belarusian) in Minsk is dedicated to the victims of the Minsk ghetto dwellers' execution specifically and the Holocaust in general. It's designed in such a way that if you decide to walk down the stairs into the pit, you'll be walked the same way that the condemned victims walked in 1942.

World War II museum in Minsk is a recently constructed modern building with an impressive exposition that was moved from an old building that was much smaller. Its exposition is well-organized, very detailed, and the tours are informative and leave a huge impression.

49

The original museum was created in the same year the war on the territory of Belarus was ended, in 1944, and it continues its mission of collecting and spreading the information about the war. You can find the information about the museum at http://www.warmuseum.by/index.php/k2-tags/k2-users/eng.

The Mound of Glory will definitely be noticed by anyone along the way from the airport to Minsk. So, in case you were wondering what that was – here's your answer. It's a memorial dedicated to Belarusian soldiers and their input into the victory of the USSR in the Great Patriotic War. This location was chosen because here's where the offensive operation "Bagration" took place in July of 1944. You can walk up the Mound, overcoming the 241 stairs (which isn't too hard for a regular adult, but might be a little complicated for children), to not only enjoy the view, but also to take a better look at the commemorative decorations in the very typical USSR style on top of it.

ETHNO-TOURISM

BELARUS SURELY HAS SOMETHING TO OFFER YOU IN THE FIELD OF ETHNO-tourism. As a country that respects its past and its traditions, it's also ready to showcase these traditions to younger generations and tourists. There are a few well-made interactive museums dedicated to this traditional old lifestyle, as well as numerous farmsteads for rent. Belarusians also organize and enjoy multiple traditional festivals and celebrations.

The Museum of Old Crafts "Dudutki" (this name sounds funny to both locals and foreigners, and it stems from the 1600's village name Dudichi) in the Minsk region stands by the Ptich river. The museum was created in 1993. It has the only ancient windmill in the country that is still working, and you can have a tour inside of it and learn how it operates. And that, surely, isn't the only thing you can witness. Among other things are blacksmithing, bread baking, various crafts, vintage cars, farm animals, brewing, and even moonshine making (with the only machine in Belarus that is officially authorized to make moonshine). The local word for moonshine is "samogon", which means "self-made alcohol". This place would be great for both adults and kids, and it's a place where you can not only watch but touch things too. And ride horses! The museum's website is http://www.dudutki.by/en/.

The Belarusian State Museum of Folk Architecture and Rural Life is located in Ozertso village, Minsk region. The museum is named Strochitcy, however, it's also often called Ozertso by the name of the village, so don't be confused – these two names are the same place. This is the so-called Skansen type of open-air museum. Strochitcy was established in 1976, and currently has a very impressive collection of interesting items, from regular to rare. The museum itself consists of six sections, but not according to the actual regions of Belarus. Instead, these are its traditional "regions", territories that were divided mostly by rivers. Each of the regions has its own architectural and cultural features that still remain to these days in terms of dialects and traditions (since current architecture is very standardized and doesn't look different anymore). So come and join the museum's guides on this fascinating journey through history and traditions. Their website is http://en.etna.by/.

Folk Arts Museum Bezdezhsky Fartushok ("the apron of Bezdezh") in the old village of Bezdezh, Brest region, is famous for its snow-white flax aprons with symbolic patterns that have been crafted there for many years. Local craftswomen had many secrets to their technology to make the fabric incredibly soft and thin. The museum offers tours that will tell stories about the everyday life of Belarusians and local folk fashion traditions. The territory of the museum also has a farm estate that offers traditional food, fishing, or cart rides.

SPORTS IN BELARUS

ONE CAN SAY THAT BELARUS IS QUITE A SPORTY COUNTRY, AND IT would be right. A lot of people have heard about Belarus thanks to the sports events that were held there. And Belarus definitely knows a thing or two about hosting sports events for foreign guests. Belarusians themselves appreciate sports too. There are multiple options to rent a bicycle almost anywhere and the biking infrastructure is getting better and better, local people love seeing hockey games and biathlon championships, spending their time at the waterparks, swimming pools, and gyms. You shouldn't give up on your health while you're there as well!

The **National Winter Olympic Training Center Raubichi in the Minsk region is considered to be one of the best biathlon training centers in the whole world. Its facilities include roller ski tracks, ski tracks, shooting grounds, indoor skating rink, several gyms, tennis courts, restaurants and cafes, a healthcare unit, and equipment** rentals. It will also offer you 4-star hotels and conference rooms, if necessary.

The **Silichi ski resort is also located in the Minsk region. It's very well-known among locals and tourists and offers a variety of services all year long. You can go there if you're a beginner, and there are special tracks for kids. Any equipment can be easily rent, and medical assistance is always near to help in case of any emergencies. You can rent a hotel room or a guest house if you want, and, apart from various skiing tracks, Silichi offers you a spa, restaurants, gyms, an extreme park, and a children's playground.**

Ratomka village near Minsk has the famous **National Olympic Training Center for Equestrian Sports and Horse Breeding, simply called Ratomka by the locals. It's not just a training ground for the professionals, it also offers sightseeing tours, horse rides and riding lessons for kids and adults, hippotherapy, and it hosts festivals and celebrations as well. The center's address is** 136 Koritskogo Street, Ratomka.

Waterparks would be really fun for an entire family. In summer, you can visit the **Dreamland Park** in Minsk, where different events are organized quite often, as well as its open-air waterpark. But in case you have any doubts about the weather, you'll be welcome in a closed waterpark. The **Lebyazhy Waterpark** in Minsk is the largest one in Belarus and the fifth largest in Europe. It offers numerous waterslides, both indoors and outdoors, a surfing simulator, spa programs, children's zones, gyms, food, and a hotel. **Freestyle Waterpark** in

Minsk is smaller, but also one-of-a-kind: along with water slides, spa, catering services, bowling, billiards, and children's zones it also has a high-technology indoor freestyle training center.

ART MUSEUMS

BELARUS HAS ALWAYS BEEN A FRUITFUL LAND FOR ART. MANY FAMOUS painters and artists were born and/or lived there throughout history, founded their own artistic communities, and gained their influence in the world of art. Today the land of Belarus keeps birthing unbelievably talented people that make life brighter and better.

The National Art Museum of the Republic of Belarus is located in Minsk. It's a true cultural treasure of the country, hosting many exhibitions and gathering both the country's artists and the tourists under its roof. 8902 square meters of art contains over 30000 items, and the electronic catalogs are being constantly updated. Of course, it doesn't only contain paintings: you can get acquainted with sculpture, wood carving, ancient iconography, and more. The museum also has its own restoration workshop with the most up-to-date equipment. You can visit https://www.artmuseum.by/eng/ to learn more and book a tour in English.

The gallery of Contemporary Art "Ў", also located in Minsk, is not just an art gallery, but a local platform for international cultural exchange. You can just call it "Y", since this letter doesn't exist in any other alphabet except Belarusian, and this is how the gallery got its name – unique, authentic, and easily recognizable. It holds exhibitions, workshops, lectures, discussions, meetings, and educational programs, and it would be a really curious place for you to visit if you're into contemporary art and want to learn more what life as an artist in modern Belarus is like. They also offer the services of art-consulting for those who are interested in purchasing artworks or even creating their private art collection (or for those who already own one). Their website with all the information and the event schedule is http://en.ygallery.by/.

The city of Vitebsk is a popular location for art lovers. It's captured in numerous paintings of the famous Belarusian avant-garde painter Marc Chagall, and the city itself is as worth visiting as the museums dedicated to the painter. **The Marc Chagall House-museum** would be a treat for his fans, but also an interesting place for those who don't know much about him. It's dedicated to the artist's family, his life, and his deep connection to Vitebsk, and it holds a collection of household articles of that time, copies of documents, and some of the paintings. **The Marc Chagall Art Center** exhibits a much larger collection of his graphic works. If you're interested, you can visit http://chagal-vitebsk.com/node/159.

Moreover, **the Vitebsk Museum of Art** and **the Vitebsk Center of Modern Art** (http://artvitebsk.museum.by/en), located across the road from one another in the city center and being very easy to find, also have impressive collections of famous artists' works and the representatives of the Vitebsk Avant-garde School, including Marc Chagall, Kazimir Malevich, Yehuda Pen, and others.

Mogilev can offer you the famous **Mogilev Regional Arts Museum** named after P.V. Maslennikov, the art collector who donated 125 works of art to this museum. The museum itself is located in the beautiful building that is an architectural monument of the early 20th century and combines several architectural styles. Inside you will find an impressive collection of paintings and other works of Belarusian art, mostly connected to the city of Mogilev itself and its art schools' techniques. The event schedule of the museum and its exposition information can be found at http://maslenikov. museum.by/en.

The art gallery of Polotsk, Vitebsk region, is housed in a former Jesuit collegium, which is the architectural monument of the 18th century. This art gallery has a large collection of religious applied arts, iconostases, secular portraits, and other Belarusian works of fine arts. The items in the exposition vary from really ancient to more modern, showing an entire history and development of fine arts in Belarus. The gallery also hosts other temporary exhibitions along with its permanent one. The collection of this museum grows constantly because the archaeological excavations are currently carried out in Polotsk, which is one of the oldest towns in the whole country. The gallery's website is http://gallery.polotsk.museum.by/en.

MUSEUMS AND PLACES DEDICATED TO
FAMOUS PEOPLE

YANKA KUPALA AND YAKUB KOLAS ALWAYS GO TOGETHER AS A
bonded pair in the minds of Belarusians. No, they weren't a romantic
couple, but they lived in the same period of time, they both were (and
still remain) very famous Belarusian poets, who wrote on similar
topics, and they also knew each other pretty close in life. Their works
are studied in schools and usually follow one another in the learning
program, and that's what makes them so inseparable in the minds of
the locals. Their museums are located in Minsk (but they are two
different buildings in different places!) and are open for visiting if you
want to dive into the lives of Belarusian poets and their lifestyle of the
20th century. While Yanka Kupala's museum (http://kupala-
museum.by/) is an exhibition with several rooms and installations,
Yakub Kolas's museum (http://kolas.museum.by/en) used to be his
actual house where he spent the last ten years of his life.

Tadeusz Kostyushko's memorial museum-estate in Kossovo, Brest
region, is dedicated to the National hero of Belarus, Poland, Lithuania,

France, and the USA – Tadeusz Kostyushko himself. The house where the exhibition is located stands in the place of the house Tadeusz was born in. It was reconstructed to become a museum, and it is now an exact copy of the old house. The exhibition is quite impressive and has the memorial and the historical part. The memorial part includes five restored rooms with the interiors of those times. The museum's website is http://kastiushka.museum.by/en.

The **Adam Mickiewicz** house-museum in Novogrudok, Grodno region, isn't just a biographical exhibition, it's an entire restored manor that includes a house, an outbuilding, a well, and a gazebo. It would be a very interesting place to visit if you love the works of the famous Polish-Belarusian poet, but it's also just a curious piece of architecture and old life. The information can be found at http://mickiewicz. museum.by/en.

There's no actual museum dedicated to Israeli politician and winner of the Nobel Peace Prize **Shimon Peres** (yet). However, in Vishnevo village (Minsk region) where he was born, you'll find a restored house of his family, marked by a memorial plaque. Peres himself remembered his homeland pretty well, he could speak Belarusian and he came to visit this village twice in his life. Despite the fact that there's no museum, the locals can pretty much tell you the entire story of Shimon Peres's life.

Ilya Repin, a well-known Russian painter, wasn't born in Belarus, but often visited his manor in Zdravnevo, Vitebsk region. This manor is now a museum dedicated to the painter's life and works. He took a big part in designing the manor, and that's what defined its unusual look. It's located in a very picturesque location as well, and this is probably the reason why the painter decided to purchase this place instead of a house near Saint Petersburg. The manor's exhibition some of Ilya Repin's personal items and some copies of his famous paintings.

Vasil Bykov was a well-known Belarusian writer, whose books were known abroad and made into movies. Vasil Bykov's museum in Bychki village, Vitebsk region, used to be his private summer cottage (the so-called "dacha"). And even though he didn't work in that house too much, because he considered that the atmosphere wasn't suitable for working, he still loved this place. It has the vibe of old times as if nothing has ever changed outside and the years have never passed. Soviet furniture, vinyl records, books, and other personal belongings of the writer won't leave you unimpressed, especially if you like retro interiors.

The memorial wall of Viktor Tsoi isn't included in any official tour guides and might seem uninteresting at first sight, yet it symbolizes a big phenomenon in the local culture. Viktor Tsoi was a huge rock-, post-punk- and new wave-star in the 1980s, the lead singer of the band named "Kino", and an actor. Despite his death in the early nineties, he remains a big influential artistic figure in post-USSR countries. His music and distinctive singing voice are still widely known and well-recognized, the lyrics that he wrote are relevant to these days, and his fans believe that he was thinking way ahead of his time. The lyrics of Kino were quite simple, yet thoughtful, and contained themes like romance, peace manifests, and desire for change.

And just the way his art reflected the local mentality and culture and the whole "post-punk" mood of that time, so does his memorial wall. In fact, it isn't a wall, but just a piece of concrete fencing that was used to surround the construction site on the central square in Minsk, and soon after Viktor's death was quickly filled with inscriptions: song quotes and goodbye words. It can serve as a work of art and a piece of history itself, even if you don't know much about the singer. It was moved from its original place and is now located on the riverbank in a small park named Lyakhovsky Square, which is located between Pervomayskaya subway station and Dynamo stadium. The city administration currently has the project of renovating the park and the memorial wall, but it's not yet certain when would it take place and whether that would happen at all.

Funny and unusual sculptures to take pictures with

It's always cool to bring non-trivial pictures from your travels, no matter if you're going to show them to anyone or not. This is why you might be interested in dropping by a statue or two if you're in town. And I don't mean the posh monuments dedicated to important people or historical dates. Some statues can showcase local culture even better.

In **Shklov** (Mogilev region) on Leninskaya street, you'll find a bronze sculpture of a character that portrays a humanized cucumber, that will remind you of Humpty Dumpty a little bit. It was placed there as a reference to a huge amount of cucumbers that are grown in Shklov yearly. The author of the statue says that this cucumber is magical, and you can try this out by rubbing the statue's pocket to attract wealth into your life.

A small statue of a sparrow (not the captain one, but a regular little bird), created with the support of the Belarusian Birdlife Protection organization, is located on Heinola Boulevard in **Baranovichi**, Brest region. It was meant to draw attention to the declining population of sparrows in Belarus. The year this sculpture was installed, 2003, was declared the year of the house sparrow.

One of the most famous, you can even say viral, statues happens to be in the town of **Bobruisk**. It's a statue of a beaver standing up straight and holding a top hat in his paw. The name Bobruisk can be translated as something similar to Beavertown, and the town's name can be considered viral because it was a big joke on the Russian-speaking segment of the Internet more than ten years ago. It was usually referred to as a place where you would tell your opponent to go if you didn't like what they were saying. So, if you want to touch a part of this culture or just take a picture with a huge bronze beaver who's wearing a vintage suit, look for it on Socialisticheskaya street, 34 in Bobruisk, Mogilev region.

Another well-recognizable sculpture can be found in **Volkovysk** (Grodno region) on Lenina street, 26. It's dedicated to two main characters of the famous Soviet animated series "Nu, Pogodi!" (known abroad as "Well, Just You Wait!". The entire series is centered around the adventures and misadventures of the Wolf character, who is always chasing the Hare character around with a purpose of eating him, but ends up never causing him any harm (kind of like in Tom & Jerry series). A curious fact is that the name of the town, Volkovysk, comes from the phrase "wolf howl" in Belarusian, and the wolf is the symbol of the town, so both of the sculpture characters appear to be in the right place there.

While being in **Grodno**, consider visiting a small sculpture of a famous fairytale character – the Traveling Frog. It's located at

Ozheshko street, 34. The frog will be a great companion for a touristic picture, because, since you got there, you're considered a traveler as well.

A really charming and lovely statue can be found right in the middle of Zvezd square in **Mogilev**, near Lepeshinskogo street. The name of the square literally means "Star Square", and it was meant to be a local equivalent of the Hollywood Walk of Fame. The square is dedicated to the famous people born or living in Mogilev, and right in the middle of it, you'll see a beautiful sculpture of Stargazer (or Astronomer) with his telescope, surrounded by twelve bronze chairs. The sculpture itself is a big sundial, and it's believed to bring you good luck and grant your wish if you make this wish sitting on the chair that fits your Zodiac sign.

Minsk has a lot to offer in the field of city sculptures as well. In Mikhaylovski square near the central railway station, you'll find three lovely human sculptures that casually blend into the surroundings. Another sculptures, well known among the locals, are located near the Komarovsky marketplace: an old woman selling sunflower seeds, a horse, a vintage photographer with his camera, and a young well-dressed lady with her little dog. Each of them would look amazing on their own or if you pair up with them for the picture. A marketplace-themed statue is located behind the Zakhodni market, portraying a villager man, who arrived at the marketplace to sell a goose and a pig. The sculpture was originally named "the Merchant" by its creator, but people quickly named this distinctive character Dzyadzka Antos' (Uncle Antos' in Belarusian). Among other interesting and beautiful sculptures that won't take too long to find and aren't too far from the city center are the ones near the building of the State Circus; four sculptures of a family that's going shopping near the TSUM store; and a sculpture of the vintage postman near the "Oktyabr" cinema building (this location isn't as random as it may seem, because there are newspaper offices located nearby). But, probably, the most popular sculpture among both locals and tourists is "the Governor's Carriage" near the Town Hall. It portrays the carriage itself with the two horses, and you can easily climb either on the horses or inside the carriage for the pictures.

ROMANTIC PLACES TO VISIT AS A COUPLE

THE BOTANICAL GARDEN IN MINSK IS AN ABSOLUTELY breathtaking place in the warm season, that also offers a year-round greenhouse with a collection of exotic plants and birds. If you are looking for a calm and quiet place to spend your day in, enjoy some strolls in the huge park, and take a lot of beautiful pictures, no matter if they're pictures of you and your partner, landscape pictures, or macro shots of the plants, the Botanical Garden is the right place for it all. Every plant has a sign near it that has all of the information about this certain species, and since the garden belongs to and is taken care of by the National Science Academy, there is a possibility to purchase some plants in the local shop, if you're interested in that. You can spend an entire day there and completely lose track of time. The admission tickets are pretty cheap and can be easily bought right at the entrance, and the garden hosts different events as well. If you want to take pictures with a more professional camera than your cell phone offers, you'll have to pay a photographer's fee, but it would be absolutely worth it.

If you're done with the garden and the day isn't over yet, you can actually continue your walk in the **Chelyuskintcev park** that is "next door" to the Botanical Garden with just the fence keeping the two of them apart. They say that if you find a fir tree there, covered in ribbons, and tie a ribbon of your own on it before making a wish, it will surely be granted. The wishes that concern your love life count as well.

Loshytsky Park in Minsk is a large and beautiful park with numerous bicycle trails, benches, small hidden locations, a beautiful riverbank and an old oak tree that is also believed to grant wishes. It's really easy to get lost in the park, but it wouldn't be dangerous for you, and you'll discover a direction marker sooner or later. There's a lovely small café in the park that serves hot beverages and sells souvenirs, and you'll also find a couple of museums not far from this café. One of them is the large manor that you can book a guided tour at (via loshytsa@gmail.com or by calling them at +375172851886), and the basement of the manor building holds a restaurant that serves traditional local food and also has the spirit of the old time that is preserved inside the manor.

The planetarium, located in the Gorky Park in Minsk, is a great place for kids, as well as the park itself, but among regular shows, it offers special shows for romantic couples as well. You can book a show in advance, not less than a week before the desired date, either via email planetarium@belastro.net or by calling them by their landline phone number: +375172943364. The building itself is a great example of Soviet architecture, and visiting it might bring you either a nostalgic feeling or an entirely new experience, but it would be worth it in any case.

The observation deck on top of the National Library in Minsk will give you a nice view of the library's surroundings, the beautiful newly built neighborhoods and the beautiful mosaics of the old Soviet buildings. These buildings were built in the 1970s and were really futuristic back in a day, and the mosaics represent Minsk as the city of war heroes, hard-working people, art, and science. It's a beautiful example of Soviet aesthetics. The library itself may be something you've heard of because its "questionable" design was widely discussed when it was built. It often can be found in the lists of the ugliest buildings in Europe, but it's highly recommended to go and see it for yourself to form your own opinion.

The Trinity Suburb in the center of Minsk is an extremely popular place for taking pictures. It's a small neighborhood of old pastel-colored houses and eye-catching cobblestones (and there aren't too many places in Belarus where you can find cobblestones out in the streets), and it's one of the most well-recognized sights of Belarus due to the fact that its pictures are often placed on souvenirs and various merchandise. But not only does it offer pretty little houses and romantic courtyards – you and your partner can also have a good time in one of the cozy cafes or tearooms, visit a museum or an arts and crafts gallery, or surprise each other with the gifts bought at the books and antiques' shop.

Janka Kupala National Theatre in Minsk and its restaurant Austeria Urshulya would be an incredible plan for a romantic evening. The restaurant is named after the daughter of Neswizh's Duke – the lady who founded theatrical art in Belarus. The menu offers you traditional dishes of Russian, Lithuanian and Belarusian cuisine. The theater itself is considered to be the best theater in the city, and rightfully so. Its repertoire is incredibly wide, and you can find any play to your taste because most of them are translated into English. Their official website, where you can see the playbill, purchase tickets, and find any other information, is https://kupalauski.by/en/.

The floating hotel Polesie, that is considered to be among the top most romantic holiday places of Belarus, is casting its anchor on the river Pripyat in the town of Turov, Gomel region. It offers comfortable tours along different waterway routes. You can admire the nature along the way, have dinners on the open deck, or go fishing.

The walking street in Brest (it's, in fact, called Sovetskaya street) is one of the bits of authentic old Europe that you can find in Belarus. There are beautiful architecture and numerous cafes and restaurants on both sides of this street, just like in popular European touristic places. And, if you're lucky enough, in the evening you and your partner can encounter the lantern-man, who lights all the lanterns in the street manually, just like the old times.

The Isle of Love on the Minsk Sea, located in the Ratomka village, can be rented for special events or just for the two of you to enjoy each other's company. Lovely gazebos, benches, and barbecue spots will be at your service, and the island itself looks really romantic, being connected to the coast with a wooden bridge. You can check out the information about the booking options at https://yunost.by/english/uslugi/arenda-besedok.

Art-Villa "Anna" in Agarki village, Minsk region, is basically a fancy hotel with breakfast, a pool, barbecue, sauna, fireplace, karaoke bar, a park, a pier in the lake, and a private beach zone. Yet, it would be an amazing opportunity to have a luxurious romantic holiday at an aesthetic homestead in the style of classical Polish houses from the beginning of the 20th century. The manor is surrounded by a beautiful forest and numerous water springs, where the Svisloch river takes its source. It will also offer you the airport transfer for some extra money, so it might actually be the only place you'll need in Belarus if you want your trip to be short, comfortable and romantic.

OTHER FAMOUS SIGHTS THAT
YOU'LL LOVE

IF YOU ARE A CAT LOVER AND YOU FOUND YOURSELF IN MINSK AMONG the old buildings around the City Hall, you can pay a visit to the **Cat Museum**. It's more of a café with themed snacks and a kitty shelter, rather than an actual museum. But it has a small gallery full of cat-related arts and crafts available for purchasing, and everything that you buy will support the museum and the animals. The place is run by people who rescue cats from the streets and gave them a place to live, and the cats that live in this museum are up for adoption. The place is perfectly suitable for children, and tea or coffee with snacks are included in the entry ticket. You can also pet cats, take pictures of them and with them, or draw something cat-themed that will be exhibited in a special room for the future guests. The museum's website with their working schedule and a list of visiting rules is at https:// catmuseum.by/index_en.html

Kilometre Zero is a small sculpture in the shape of a pyramid that is located on Oktyabrskaya Square in Minsk. To be honest, that's the only thing that is located on this square, except for the looming Palace of the Republic and possible temporary setups for national holidays. The Palace of the Republic is sometimes called "the sarcophagus" within the architectural circles and the locals because of its shape and design – a good example of Soviet architecture. But let's get back to Kilometre Zero. As the sculptures of this type usually do, it shows how many kilometers there are to various points of the world from this exact point. Sometimes it can be quite fascinating to think about your place on Earth, especially during your travels. Besides, it's a very notable location that you can take a good picture with.

The City Gate is almost the first thing that greets you when you step outside the main entrance of the central railway station in Minsk, and it's clearly visible from the central bus station too. This location is easily recognizable due to its presence on numerous pictures and souvenirs. And even though it's called the gate, it's just two towers of regular apartment buildings, separated by a street. They stand in perfect symmetry to the square's transversal axis, and that is the reason why they look so fascinating. It's most likely that they were named the City Gate because they're supposed to be the first thing you should see upon arriving in Minsk. The towers are eleven floors tall, connected to five-floor buildings on the sides. All of these buildings were built in the late 1940s and, therefore, are a perfect example of the so-called Stalinist architectural style. One of the two towers of the City Gate has the biggest German clock in the whole country on top of it. The other one has the national emblem of Belarusian SSR, a nonexistent at present time country, in the same place. Both of them are also decorated with several sculptures, that aren't from the 1940s but are the exact reconstructed copies of the original ones.

.   .   .

71

The National Historical Museum is located in Minsk and is, probably, the most famous museum in the entire country. It was founded in 1914 and originally dedicated to religion and archaeology, but during Soviet times and after that, it has changed its name and topic several times. In 2012 the current exhibition of the museum was finally completed, and now contains thousands of items, some of them have not only local but global significance. The museum also hosts temporary exhibitions. The museum's website is http://histmuseum.by/en/.

Leninskaya street in Mogilev is an old and beautiful pedestrian-only street that consists of buildings dating back to the 18th-19th centuries. It will surely give you a historical vibe of old Europe and provide you with numerous locations to take pictures nearby. You can also have a meal or a cup of coffee in any of the cafes that are located on this street.

The Kamenets Tower in the Brest region is a unique specimen of defense architecture of the 13th century. The 30 m tall building will remind you of a chess rook. There was even a legend that it was built by a giant. It looks minimalistic, having no decorations, its only windows are the lancet holes, and this is what makes this tower so fascinating. It has five "floors", even though they're much taller than regular living floors, and you can go inside of it and climb all the way up to the roof, which is an observation platform now. There's also a museum inside the tower.

. . .

You may have heard of the White Tower ("Belaya Vezha" in Belarusian), the legendary tower that gave its name to Belovezhskaya Pushcha. It's a famous brand in Belarus, and there are sanatoriums, hotels, casinos, food products, and even a theater festival under that brand name. The Kamenets Tower is also referred to as the White Tower despite the fact that it has always been brick red. People started calling it that way after the author of the book about Belovezhskaya Pushcha mistakenly wrote that the tower is located on the White River. However, scientists believe that there has been another tower that gave its name to the Pushcha.

Augustow Canal is located in the Grodno region, close to the border with Poland. It was a truly unique installation back at the time when it was built due to its size and the complexion of its engineering solutions. It was constructed in the 19th century and served as transport waterway for cargo ships for some time, but later the demand for it was reduced due to the development of the railroad system. However, it became a touristic attraction and a hiking place as early as the year 1909. Despite it being moderately destroyed during the two wars, it has later been restored and now you can take a tour along the canal and see these magnificent retro machines in use. You can also hike, rent a boat, a bicycle, or a gazebo for barbecuing. The location of the Canal was very suitable for military defense installations, and you can find several of them nearby and on the way to the Canal.

The Museum of the Belarusian book-printing in Polotsk, Vitebsk region, is located in a building that is an architectural monument of the 18th century itself. The museum contains over 2500 rare items on display in 15 well-designed rooms, and it will tell you a

73

story of the development of Belarusian book-printing from the first manuscripts to what we see today as current books. The place isn't strictly about books - you will like it here if you're a stationery lover or if you enjoy ancient postcards and calendars.

The town of Zaslavl, Minsk region, is one of the oldest towns in the entire country. It's quite small and you can easily get there by taking an electric train from Minsk. The railway station is named "Belarus" because it used to be the last station on the border with Poland a long time ago. And this town, especially its historical central part, is absolutely worth visiting because of its architecture and atmosphere. The legend of this town is connected to the famous wayward Princess Rogneda, who was forcibly married to the Duke Vladimir of Kiev himself, and she hated it so much that she attempted to kill him. This attempt failed, and the punishment should have been that Vladimir now kills her, however, their young son Izyaslav defended his mother with a sword. That was the reason why both of them were banished to this town, which was named after Izyaslav, and the name turned into Zaslavl. You'll find the old castle's ruins, a few churches, several historical museums, statues, and fortifications there. The so-called Minsk Sea is also located nearby.

Yurovichi village in the Gomel region would be a gem for those who love archaeology and really ancient settlements. One of the oldest well-preserved primeval settlements was found in this beautiful village. Another feature of this location is the high hills around the village and the old berm that's left of the ancient wooden castle that once stood there. The place used to be a very huge trading post, that's why it needed protection. So if your heart skips a beat when you think of how much history the places can contain – Yurovichi is a destination for you.

MISCELLANEOUS TIPS AND FACTS

GHOST STORIES

There are actually many legends and ghost stories in Belarus, that are mostly centered around the ghosts of young girls that died mysteriously. Almost every old manor or castle has its own legend or even a few of them. Sometimes the old legends are used on purpose to create the atmosphere around the place and attract more curious tourists and locals (for examples, the legends of the famous castles, that are told during tours and sometimes included into the theatrical shows that are put on for the visitors as part of the castle tours). But some of the stories aren't very well-known even among the locals. Not too many people know the story about the ghost of Kalvaryyskoye graveyard. The legend says that in late nights in November if you come close to the graveyard chapel, you can see a ghost of a young lady, whose body was buried alive a long time ago by mistake. However, this story isn't true – both in terms of the lady's burial (there is no such grave anywhere near the chapel) and in terms of the ghostly presence. Another rare story is about a ghost of a young lady that can be seen in

Loshytsky park in Minsk during spring nights when the moon is full. The legend speaks about the owners of the park and the manor, and their unhappy marriage. There's a belief that if you encounter that ghost of the last owner's wife on the bank of the river near the manor, she's able to give you a piece of advice on your love life.

Ghost stories are, surely, always sad, because, according to the common beliefs, one has to die in a terrible way and never find their peace in order to become a ghost. But these legends can also add some mystical aura to the place and emphasize its long and impressive history. Even though there is no proof whatsoever if there was any real-life inspiration behind any of these legends or not.

Superstitions

The older generation of Belarusians, especially in the villages, widely believes in all kinds of superstitions. That is one of the reasons why various good luck charms are popular souvenirs, and why some traditions and rituals exist the way they are. Some of the superstitions are really absurd, but local people are so used to them that they would expect you to do the same way. For example, whistling inside the house is bad luck, because you'll whistle away all the money. It's a really bad sign if you greet someone over the doorstep – so, they would expect you to either let the person in first or step outside yourself. This superstition stems from ancient times when people buried their family members under the doorsteps of their houses. To have a safe trip, you have to sit down before leaving your home for a minute or two. And if your nose is itching, that means you're going to have a drink soon (presumably, alcohol).

77

. . .

What to bring as a gift to Belarusians?

If you're invited to Belarusians' home as a guest, you would probably have a question – what should you bring them? The local tradition really says that coming to someone's house with empty hands isn't polite unless these people are your best friends and you visit them every other weekend, of course. But if it's a more formal gathering – you'll need a gift.

The most classical gifts probably are high-quality alcohol, wine or liquor, and/or chocolate candies. Another classical option is a cake or any other nicely packed dessert. Most people in Belarus aren't vegan, especially the older generations, so don't worry too much about your gifts being not vegan-friendly. If the family has children, it would be nice to bring a small toy or a hypo-allergenic snack for the kids. If you're still unsure whether edible items are a good option in your case, you can bring them a bed linen set or a set of kitchen towels – another traditionally valued gift option. A nice souvenir from your home country or a good-looking decorative item for their home would make a great gift as well.

Don't drink tap water

The level of water purity varies from one country region to another (it can vary noticeably even within one city), due to the soil type and quality, the location of industrial factories, and other factors. But no matter where you are in Belarus, drinking tap water isn't recommended unless the water is filtered. Hotels and highly rated apartments should have water filters pre-installed into the taps, at least in the kitchen, but you might need to buy bottled water to drink if you're staying in a less fancy place. You might need a little more hair conditioner and skin moisturizer than usual if your body is used to the water with less chlorine in it.

How much of a tip to leave for the waiters?

Unlike many other countries, tips for the staff aren't that much of a thing in Belarus, they are never included in the bills, and most people, unfortunately, never bother to leave any tips at all. Of course, the staff would very much appreciate it if you tip them because it's a nice bonus for their regular salary. Those who work in the service industry tend to say that foreign tourists leave many more tips than locals do. That's because things and practices that are common for the most advanced countries come to Belarus quite slowly and reluctantly.

So, if you're traveling on a tight budget and don't have any extra money to tip the staff, you don't have to stress about it, because everybody is quite used to it, and you won't get any angry looks. Just be polite. But if you decide to leave a tip for your waiter or bartender, you will indeed make them happier. The "required" percentage of tips isn't regulated by any official (or unofficial) rules, therefore you can give as much as you want.

. . .

Don't jaywalk

Some countries have pretty calm road traffic even in their capital cities, so you can see their local people casually jaywalking here and there. But Belarusian people can be recognized abroad by the fact that they will most likely stand in front of an empty road, stubbornly waiting for the green light. Jaywalking in Belarus isn't just illegal, it's also extremely unsafe, because the traffic is quite busy, and local drivers can be wild. So please don't attempt that. Small towns and villages can be exceptions, but always check the road before you go.

What if you're gay?

Same-sex partnerships are currently decriminalized in Belarus, even though they're not accepted by the government. The younger generation of Belarusians has more open-minded views on sexuality and tolerance, but most of the locals still have very "traditional" (i.e. homophobic) worldviews. You won't feel Western Europe-like, relaxed attitude towards non-straight people from every person that you meet. If you're in the same-sex relationship and traveling with your partner, it would be best for you to avoid public displays of affection and book twin rooms with two beds rather than rooms with a single bed. Local citizens, especially people of older generations, can sometimes be overly curious.

Don't support street merchants

. . .

Street merchants, the ones who bring their own chairs and display their goods on cardboard boxes, are quite a common thing in Belarus. While what they do is officially considered illegal, no one tries really hard to effectively get rid of them. Most of them sell pretty innocent things, from homegrown vegetables and sunflower seeds to hairclips. They don't pose any threat, but no matter who the particular merchant is – a part of an organized clandestine business or just a person trying to earn some extra money – it wouldn't be a good thing to support them financially. However, if you decide to do so – do that at your own risk, since it's most likely that no one of them speaks English.

Stores' working time

Belarus is a country where you can easily find a store that works late in the evening, no matter if it's a corner shop or a supermarket. The vast majority of stores and pharmacies work up until the evening and during weekends, and stores that work around the clock aren't too hard to find in big cities as well. Therefore, you won't have to stress about stocking up on food before the weekend, and you won't run out of supplies no matter when you arrive in Belarus. Small shops in smaller towns may have a shorter working day, but most of the towns have typical chain supermarkets in them.

Hot water shutdown

If you come to Belarus in the summer and you're staying in a rented apartment, via CouchSurfing, or at someone's private home in general, you might have a chance to experience a typical two-week hot water shutdown. Most apartments and houses are fitted with their own water heaters so that the inhabitants won't have to depend on these shutdowns, but some people just like it rough and heat their bathing water in huge pots. Why does that happen? This is a part of the regional water system maintenance routine. Hot water in Belarus is centrally heated and pumped to the houses individually through the pipe system. The workers must maintain and clean the hot water system to prepare it for the winter season, and during the maintenance period (about two weeks) hot water is turned off completely. The locals can check the water shutdown dates for their particular neighborhood in advance online, and those who don't use the internet will find out about the shutdown a few days before it happens when the announcement paper appears on the house entrance.

Smoking and drinking in public places

Drinking any kind of alcoholic beverages in public places is forbidden by the law. Of course, we don't count bars or restaurants where you can buy and consume alcohol. But if any militiaman will catch you drinking on the street or in the park, this will get you in trouble. Just so you know, the militiamen can be out there patrolling the area even if it's far from the city center, especially during holidays and public celebrations.

Smoking is also prohibited in most public places, including bus stops, and you'll have to find a spot that's specifically marked to be a smoking area, or just move far enough from the "no smoking" sign. But there are lots of bars, restaurants, and cafes that allow smoking inside.

. . .

Overcoming the language barrier

Since Belarus has two official languages, some signs are printed in Russian, while some are in Belarusian. Those who are responsible for doing it and are supposed to ensure comfortable orienteering, unfortunately, don't know English very well most of the time, so there might be some misunderstandings or translation errors due to the usage of automatic translation. Other difficulties may be caused by the fact that most of the signs that are meant for tourists are being transcribed from Belarusian rather than translated. So it would be best for you to keep an online or offline translation app and an interactive map nearby.

Useful websites and apps for travelers

https://airport.by/en is the official website of the Minsk National Airport with all of the necessary information that you might need.

Goes is the free transport app for iOS and Android. It supports several cities and you can choose the English language in the settings.

MinskRoutes is a free iOS app for public transport schedules and routes.

Yandex Maps, available for both Android and iOS, is a free map that works the best in Belarus, knowing its way around the smallest streets and towns. You can also download a GPS navigator made by the same developers.

KrokApp is an app for Android that offers audio guides through the biggest Belarusian cities.

KOLOBIKE is a free bike-sharing app for Android and iOS. This kind of service is something new for Belarus, it was established very recently, and it's not as widespread as it is in other European countries, however, it's working well, and you can use it too.

Menu.by is a free app for Android and iOS that will help you with the food delivery and takeaway meals in Minsk. It works with most major restaurants so that you won't have to study them all separately.

https://www.belarus.by/en/ is the official website of Belarus, with all the freshest news and the official info about visas and travel documents.

http://law.by/ is the website about Belarusian state laws and the newest updates in them.

https://vetliva.com/ is a website dedicated to famous local sights, their locations and descriptions. All of the information is available in English.

. . .

https://34travel.me/gotobelarus/en is another website about Belarusian landmarks, made with love and style.

http://hifivebelarus.com/ is a project made by locals for foreigners who want to travel to Belarus and get the most out of their travels.

http://www.etobelarusdetka.com/english1 and http://www.etobelarusdetka.com/english is a curious blog about daily life in Belarus and how it's different from other cultures. The authors of this blog released their own book "This is Belarus, babe!" that can be easily purchased online or in several bookstores.

CPSIA information can be obtained
at www.ICGtesting.com
Printed in the USA
BVHW030325020822
643544BV00021B/2089